this bucket list
belongs to

_____

_____

"never give up because great things take time"

OUR BUCKET LIST

WE WANT TO DO THIS BECAUSE

_____

_____

_____

_____

OUR MEMORIES AND THOUGHTS

_____

_____

_____

_____

_____

_____

_____

_____

_____

COMPLETION DATE

_____

WOULD WE DO IT AGAIN?   YES ☐   NO ☐

OUR BUCKET LIST

WE WANT TO DO THIS BECAUSE

OUR MEMORIES AND THOUGHTS

COMPLETION DATE

WOULD WE DO IT AGAIN?   YES ☐   NO ☐

OUR BUCKET LIST

WE WANT TO DO THIS BECAUSE

OUR MEMORIES AND THOUGHTS

COMPLETION DATE

WOULD WE DO IT AGAIN?   YES ☐   NO ☐

OUR BUCKET LIST

WE WANT TO DO THIS BECAUSE

_____

_____

_____

_____

OUR MEMORIES AND THOUGHTS

_____

_____

_____

_____

_____

_____

_____

_____

COMPLETION DATE

_____

WOULD WE DO IT AGAIN?   YES ☐   NO ☐

OUR BUCKET LIST

WE WANT TO DO THIS BECAUSE

OUR MEMORIES AND THOUGHTS

COMPLETION DATE

WOULD WE DO IT AGAIN? YES ☐ NO ☐

OUR BUCKET LIST

WE WANT TO DO THIS BECAUSE

_____
_____
_____
_____

OUR MEMORIES AND THOUGHTS

_____
_____
_____
_____
_____
_____
_____
_____

COMPLETION DATE

_____

WOULD WE DO IT AGAIN?   YES ☐   NO ☐

OUR BUCKET LIST

WE WANT TO DO THIS BECAUSE

OUR MEMORIES AND THOUGHTS

COMPLETION DATE

WOULD WE DO IT AGAIN?   YES ☐   NO ☐

OUR BUCKET LIST

WE WANT TO DO THIS BECAUSE

OUR MEMORIES AND THOUGHTS

COMPLETION DATE

WOULD WE DO IT AGAIN?   YES ☐   NO ☐

OUR BUCKET LIST

WE WANT TO DO THIS BECAUSE

OUR MEMORIES AND THOUGHTS

COMPLETION DATE

WOULD WE DO IT AGAIN?   YES ☐   NO ☐

OUR BUCKET LIST

WE WANT TO DO THIS BECAUSE

_____
_____
_____
_____

OUR MEMORIES AND THOUGHTS

_____
_____
_____
_____
_____
_____
_____
_____

COMPLETION DATE

_____

WOULD WE DO IT AGAIN?　　YES ☐　　NO ☐

OUR BUCKET LIST

WE WANT TO DO THIS BECAUSE

_____

_____

_____

_____

OUR MEMORIES AND THOUGHTS

_____

_____

_____

_____

_____

_____

_____

_____

_____

COMPLETION DATE

_____

WOULD WE DO IT AGAIN?   YES ☐   NO ☐

OUR BUCKET LIST

WE WANT TO DO THIS BECAUSE

OUR MEMORIES AND THOUGHTS

COMPLETION DATE

WOULD WE DO IT AGAIN?   YES ☐   NO ☐

OUR BUCKET LIST

WE WANT TO DO THIS BECAUSE

OUR MEMORIES AND THOUGHTS

COMPLETION DATE

WOULD WE DO IT AGAIN?   YES ☐   NO ☐

OUR BUCKET LIST

WE WANT TO DO THIS BECAUSE

OUR MEMORIES AND THOUGHTS

COMPLETION DATE

WOULD WE DO IT AGAIN?   YES ☐   NO ☐

OUR BUCKET LIST

WE WANT TO DO THIS BECAUSE

OUR MEMORIES AND THOUGHTS

COMPLETION DATE

WOULD WE DO IT AGAIN?   YES ☐   NO ☐

OUR BUCKET LIST

WE WANT TO DO THIS BECAUSE

_____

_____

_____

_____

OUR MEMORIES AND THOUGHTS

_____

_____

_____

_____

_____

_____

_____

_____

COMPLETION DATE

_____

WOULD WE DO IT AGAIN?   YES ☐   NO ☐

OUR BUCKET LIST

WE WANT TO DO THIS BECAUSE

OUR MEMORIES AND THOUGHTS

COMPLETION DATE

WOULD WE DO IT AGAIN?   YES ☐   NO ☐

OUR BUCKET LIST

WE WANT TO DO THIS BECAUSE

_____

_____

_____

_____

OUR MEMORIES AND THOUGHTS

_____

_____

_____

_____

_____

_____

_____

_____

_____

COMPLETION DATE

_____

WOULD WE DO IT AGAIN? YES ☐ NO ☐

OUR BUCKET LIST

WE WANT TO DO THIS BECAUSE

_____
_____
_____
_____

OUR MEMORIES AND THOUGHTS

_____
_____
_____
_____
_____
_____
_____
_____

COMPLETION DATE

_____

WOULD WE DO IT AGAIN?   YES ☐   NO ☐

OUR BUCKET LIST

WE WANT TO DO THIS BECAUSE

OUR MEMORIES AND THOUGHTS

COMPLETION DATE

WOULD WE DO IT AGAIN?   YES ☐   NO ☐

OUR BUCKET LIST

WE WANT TO DO THIS BECAUSE

OUR MEMORIES AND THOUGHTS

COMPLETION DATE

WOULD WE DO IT AGAIN?   YES ☐   NO ☐

OUR BUCKET LIST

WE WANT TO DO THIS BECAUSE

OUR MEMORIES AND THOUGHTS

COMPLETION DATE

WOULD WE DO IT AGAIN?　　YES ☐　　NO ☐

OUR BUCKET LIST

WE WANT TO DO THIS BECAUSE

OUR MEMORIES AND THOUGHTS

COMPLETION DATE

WOULD WE DO IT AGAIN?   YES ☐   NO ☐

OUR BUCKET LIST

WE WANT TO DO THIS BECAUSE

_____
_____
_____
_____

OUR MEMORIES AND THOUGHTS

_____
_____
_____
_____
_____
_____
_____
_____

COMPLETION DATE

_____

WOULD WE DO IT AGAIN?   YES ☐   NO ☐

OUR BUCKET LIST

WE WANT TO DO THIS BECAUSE

_____

_____

_____

_____

OUR MEMORIES AND THOUGHTS

_____

_____

_____

_____

_____

_____

_____

_____

_____

COMPLETION DATE

_____

WOULD WE DO IT AGAIN?   YES ☐   NO ☐

OUR BUCKET LIST

WE WANT TO DO THIS BECAUSE

_____

_____

_____

_____

OUR MEMORIES AND THOUGHTS

_____

_____

_____

_____

_____

_____

_____

_____

COMPLETION DATE

_____

WOULD WE DO IT AGAIN?   YES ☐   NO ☐

OUR BUCKET LIST

WE WANT TO DO THIS BECAUSE

OUR MEMORIES AND THOUGHTS

COMPLETION DATE

WOULD WE DO IT AGAIN?   YES ☐   NO ☐

OUR BUCKET LIST

WE WANT TO DO THIS BECAUSE

_____
_____
_____
_____

OUR MEMORIES AND THOUGHTS

_____
_____
_____
_____
_____
_____
_____
_____

COMPLETION DATE

_____

WOULD WE DO IT AGAIN?   YES ☐   NO ☐

OUR BUCKET LIST

WE WANT TO DO THIS BECAUSE

_____

_____

_____

_____

OUR MEMORIES AND THOUGHTS

_____

_____

_____

_____

_____

_____

_____

_____

_____

COMPLETION DATE

_____

WOULD WE DO IT AGAIN?   YES ☐   NO ☐

OUR BUCKET LIST

WE WANT TO DO THIS BECAUSE

OUR MEMORIES AND THOUGHTS

COMPLETION DATE

WOULD WE DO IT AGAIN?   YES ☐   NO ☐

OUR BUCKET LIST

WE WANT TO DO THIS BECAUSE

OUR MEMORIES AND THOUGHTS

COMPLETION DATE

WOULD WE DO IT AGAIN?   YES ☐   NO ☐

OUR BUCKET LIST

WE WANT TO DO THIS BECAUSE

OUR MEMORIES AND THOUGHTS

COMPLETION DATE

WOULD WE DO IT AGAIN?   YES ☐   NO ☐

OUR BUCKET LIST

WE WANT TO DO THIS BECAUSE

OUR MEMORIES AND THOUGHTS

COMPLETION DATE

WOULD WE DO IT AGAIN?　　YES ☐　　NO ☐

OUR BUCKET LIST

WE WANT TO DO THIS BECAUSE

OUR MEMORIES AND THOUGHTS

COMPLETION DATE

WOULD WE DO IT AGAIN?   YES ☐   NO ☐

OUR BUCKET LIST

WE WANT TO DO THIS BECAUSE

_____

_____

_____

_____

OUR MEMORIES AND THOUGHTS

_____

_____

_____

_____

_____

_____

_____

_____

COMPLETION DATE

_____

WOULD WE DO IT AGAIN?   YES ☐   NO ☐

OUR BUCKET LIST

WE WANT TO DO THIS BECAUSE

_____

_____

_____

_____

OUR MEMORIES AND THOUGHTS

_____

_____

_____

_____

_____

_____

_____

_____

COMPLETION DATE

_____

WOULD WE DO IT AGAIN?   YES ☐   NO ☐

OUR BUCKET LIST

WE WANT TO DO THIS BECAUSE

OUR MEMORIES AND THOUGHTS

COMPLETION DATE

WOULD WE DO IT AGAIN?   YES ☐   NO ☐

OUR BUCKET LIST

WE WANT TO DO THIS BECAUSE

OUR MEMORIES AND THOUGHTS

COMPLETION DATE

WOULD WE DO IT AGAIN?   YES ☐   NO ☐

OUR BUCKET LIST

WE WANT TO DO THIS BECAUSE

OUR MEMORIES AND THOUGHTS

COMPLETION DATE

WOULD WE DO IT AGAIN?   YES ☐   NO ☐

OUR BUCKET LIST

WE WANT TO DO THIS BECAUSE

OUR MEMORIES AND THOUGHTS

COMPLETION DATE

WOULD WE DO IT AGAIN?   YES ☐   NO ☐

OUR BUCKET LIST

WE WANT TO DO THIS BECAUSE

_____

_____

_____

_____

OUR MEMORIES AND THOUGHTS

_____

_____

_____

_____

_____

_____

_____

_____

_____

COMPLETION DATE

_____

WOULD WE DO IT AGAIN?　　YES ☐　　NO ☐

OUR BUCKET LIST

WE WANT TO DO THIS BECAUSE

OUR MEMORIES AND THOUGHTS

COMPLETION DATE

WOULD WE DO IT AGAIN? YES ☐ NO ☐

OUR BUCKET LIST

WE WANT TO DO THIS BECAUSE

_____

_____

_____

_____

OUR MEMORIES AND THOUGHTS

_____

_____

_____

_____

_____

_____

_____

_____

COMPLETION DATE

_____

WOULD WE DO IT AGAIN?   YES ☐   NO ☐

OUR BUCKET LIST

WE WANT TO DO THIS BECAUSE

OUR MEMORIES AND THOUGHTS

COMPLETION DATE

WOULD WE DO IT AGAIN?   YES ☐   NO ☐

OUR BUCKET LIST

WE WANT TO DO THIS BECAUSE

OUR MEMORIES AND THOUGHTS

COMPLETION DATE

WOULD WE DO IT AGAIN?   YES ☐   NO ☐

OUR BUCKET LIST

WE WANT TO DO THIS BECAUSE

OUR MEMORIES AND THOUGHTS

COMPLETION DATE

WOULD WE DO IT AGAIN?   YES ☐   NO ☐

OUR BUCKET LIST

WE WANT TO DO THIS BECAUSE

OUR MEMORIES AND THOUGHTS

COMPLETION DATE

WOULD WE DO IT AGAIN?   YES ☐   NO ☐

OUR BUCKET LIST

WE WANT TO DO THIS BECAUSE

_____

_____

_____

_____

OUR MEMORIES AND THOUGHTS

_____

_____

_____

_____

_____

_____

_____

_____

COMPLETION DATE

_____

WOULD WE DO IT AGAIN?   YES ☐   NO ☐

OUR BUCKET LIST

WE WANT TO DO THIS BECAUSE

_____

OUR MEMORIES AND THOUGHTS

_____

COMPLETION DATE

_____

WOULD WE DO IT AGAIN?   YES ☐   NO ☐

OUR BUCKET LIST

WE WANT TO DO THIS BECAUSE

OUR MEMORIES AND THOUGHTS

COMPLETION DATE

WOULD WE DO IT AGAIN? YES ☐ NO ☐

OUR BUCKET LIST

WE WANT TO DO THIS BECAUSE

OUR MEMORIES AND THOUGHTS

COMPLETION DATE

WOULD WE DO IT AGAIN?   YES ☐   NO ☐

OUR BUCKET LIST

WE WANT TO DO THIS BECAUSE

OUR MEMORIES AND THOUGHTS

COMPLETION DATE

WOULD WE DO IT AGAIN? YES ☐ NO ☐

OUR BUCKET LIST

WE WANT TO DO THIS BECAUSE

OUR MEMORIES AND THOUGHTS

COMPLETION DATE

WOULD WE DO IT AGAIN?   YES ☐   NO ☐

OUR BUCKET LIST

WE WANT TO DO THIS BECAUSE

_____

_____

_____

_____

OUR MEMORIES AND THOUGHTS

_____

_____

_____

_____

_____

_____

_____

_____

_____

COMPLETION DATE

_____

WOULD WE DO IT AGAIN?   YES ☐   NO ☐

OUR BUCKET LIST

WE WANT TO DO THIS BECAUSE

OUR MEMORIES AND THOUGHTS

COMPLETION DATE

WOULD WE DO IT AGAIN?   YES ☐   NO ☐

OUR BUCKET LIST

WE WANT TO DO THIS BECAUSE

_____

_____

_____

_____

OUR MEMORIES AND THOUGHTS

_____

_____

_____

_____

_____

_____

_____

_____

COMPLETION DATE

_____

WOULD WE DO IT AGAIN?   YES ☐   NO ☐

OUR BUCKET LIST

WE WANT TO DO THIS BECAUSE

OUR MEMORIES AND THOUGHTS

COMPLETION DATE

WOULD WE DO IT AGAIN?   YES ☐   NO ☐

OUR BUCKET LIST

WE WANT TO DO THIS BECAUSE

_____

_____

_____

_____

OUR MEMORIES AND THOUGHTS

_____

_____

_____

_____

_____

_____

_____

_____

COMPLETION DATE

_____

WOULD WE DO IT AGAIN?   YES ☐   NO ☐

OUR BUCKET LIST

WE WANT TO DO THIS BECAUSE

_____

_____

_____

_____

OUR MEMORIES AND THOUGHTS

_____

_____

_____

_____

_____

_____

_____

_____

_____

COMPLETION DATE

_____

WOULD WE DO IT AGAIN?   YES ☐   NO ☐

OUR BUCKET LIST

WE WANT TO DO THIS BECAUSE

OUR MEMORIES AND THOUGHTS

COMPLETION DATE

WOULD WE DO IT AGAIN?   YES ☐   NO ☐

OUR BUCKET LIST

WE WANT TO DO THIS BECAUSE

_____

_____

_____

_____

OUR MEMORIES AND THOUGHTS

_____

_____

_____

_____

_____

_____

_____

_____

_____

_____

COMPLETION DATE

_____

WOULD WE DO IT AGAIN?   YES ☐   NO ☐

OUR BUCKET LIST

WE WANT TO DO THIS BECAUSE

OUR MEMORIES AND THOUGHTS

COMPLETION DATE

WOULD WE DO IT AGAIN?   YES ☐   NO ☐

OUR BUCKET LIST

WE WANT TO DO THIS BECAUSE

_____
_____
_____
_____

OUR MEMORIES AND THOUGHTS

_____
_____
_____
_____
_____
_____
_____
_____
_____

COMPLETION DATE

_____

WOULD WE DO IT AGAIN?   YES ☐   NO ☐

OUR BUCKET LIST

WE WANT TO DO THIS BECAUSE

_____

_____

_____

_____

OUR MEMORIES AND THOUGHTS

_____

_____

_____

_____

_____

_____

_____

_____

COMPLETION DATE

_____

WOULD WE DO IT AGAIN?　　YES ☐　　NO ☐

OUR BUCKET LIST

WE WANT TO DO THIS BECAUSE

OUR MEMORIES AND THOUGHTS

COMPLETION DATE

WOULD WE DO IT AGAIN?   YES ☐   NO ☐

OUR BUCKET LIST

WE WANT TO DO THIS BECAUSE

OUR MEMORIES AND THOUGHTS

COMPLETION DATE

WOULD WE DO IT AGAIN?   YES ☐   NO ☐

OUR BUCKET LIST

WE WANT TO DO THIS BECAUSE

OUR MEMORIES AND THOUGHTS

COMPLETION DATE

WOULD WE DO IT AGAIN?   YES ☐   NO ☐

OUR BUCKET LIST

WE WANT TO DO THIS BECAUSE

_____

_____

_____

_____

OUR MEMORIES AND THOUGHTS

_____

_____

_____

_____

_____

_____

_____

_____

_____

COMPLETION DATE

_____

WOULD WE DO IT AGAIN?   YES ☐   NO ☐

OUR BUCKET LIST

WE WANT TO DO THIS BECAUSE

OUR MEMORIES AND THOUGHTS

COMPLETION DATE

WOULD WE DO IT AGAIN? YES ☐ NO ☐

OUR BUCKET LIST

WE WANT TO DO THIS BECAUSE

_____

_____

_____

_____

OUR MEMORIES AND THOUGHTS

_____

_____

_____

_____

_____

_____

_____

_____

COMPLETION DATE

_____

WOULD WE DO IT AGAIN?   YES ☐   NO ☐

OUR BUCKET LIST

WE WANT TO DO THIS BECAUSE

_____

_____

_____

_____

OUR MEMORIES AND THOUGHTS

_____

_____

_____

_____

_____

_____

_____

_____

_____

COMPLETION DATE

_____

WOULD WE DO IT AGAIN?   YES ☐   NO ☐

OUR BUCKET LIST

WE WANT TO DO THIS BECAUSE

OUR MEMORIES AND THOUGHTS

COMPLETION DATE

WOULD WE DO IT AGAIN? YES ☐ NO ☐

OUR BUCKET LIST

WE WANT TO DO THIS BECAUSE

OUR MEMORIES AND THOUGHTS

COMPLETION DATE

WOULD WE DO IT AGAIN? YES ☐ NO ☐

OUR BUCKET LIST

WE WANT TO DO THIS BECAUSE

OUR MEMORIES AND THOUGHTS

COMPLETION DATE

WOULD WE DO IT AGAIN?   YES ☐   NO ☐

OUR BUCKET LIST

WE WANT TO DO THIS BECAUSE

OUR MEMORIES AND THOUGHTS

COMPLETION DATE

WOULD WE DO IT AGAIN?   YES ☐   NO ☐

OUR BUCKET LIST

WE WANT TO DO THIS BECAUSE

OUR MEMORIES AND THOUGHTS

COMPLETION DATE

WOULD WE DO IT AGAIN?   YES ☐   NO ☐

OUR BUCKET LIST

WE WANT TO DO THIS BECAUSE

OUR MEMORIES AND THOUGHTS

COMPLETION DATE

WOULD WE DO IT AGAIN?   YES ☐   NO ☐

OUR BUCKET LIST

WE WANT TO DO THIS BECAUSE

OUR MEMORIES AND THOUGHTS

COMPLETION DATE

WOULD WE DO IT AGAIN?　　YES ☐　　NO ☐

OUR BUCKET LIST

WE WANT TO DO THIS BECAUSE

OUR MEMORIES AND THOUGHTS

COMPLETION DATE

WOULD WE DO IT AGAIN?   YES ☐   NO ☐

OUR BUCKET LIST

WE WANT TO DO THIS BECAUSE

OUR MEMORIES AND THOUGHTS

COMPLETION DATE

WOULD WE DO IT AGAIN?   YES ☐   NO ☐

OUR BUCKET LIST

WE WANT TO DO THIS BECAUSE

OUR MEMORIES AND THOUGHTS

COMPLETION DATE

WOULD WE DO IT AGAIN?   YES ☐   NO ☐

OUR BUCKET LIST

WE WANT TO DO THIS BECAUSE

OUR MEMORIES AND THOUGHTS

COMPLETION DATE

WOULD WE DO IT AGAIN?   YES ☐   NO ☐

OUR BUCKET LIST

WE WANT TO DO THIS BECAUSE

OUR MEMORIES AND THOUGHTS

COMPLETION DATE

WOULD WE DO IT AGAIN?   YES ☐   NO ☐

OUR BUCKET LIST

WE WANT TO DO THIS BECAUSE

OUR MEMORIES AND THOUGHTS

COMPLETION DATE

WOULD WE DO IT AGAIN?   YES ☐   NO ☐

OUR BUCKET LIST

WE WANT TO DO THIS BECAUSE

OUR MEMORIES AND THOUGHTS

COMPLETION DATE

WOULD WE DO IT AGAIN?   YES ☐   NO ☐

OUR BUCKET LIST

WE WANT TO DO THIS BECAUSE

OUR MEMORIES AND THOUGHTS

COMPLETION DATE

WOULD WE DO IT AGAIN?   YES ☐   NO ☐

OUR BUCKET LIST

WE WANT TO DO THIS BECAUSE

_____

_____

_____

_____

OUR MEMORIES AND THOUGHTS

_____

_____

_____

_____

_____

_____

_____

_____

COMPLETION DATE

_____

WOULD WE DO IT AGAIN?　　YES ☐　　NO ☐

OUR BUCKET LIST

WE WANT TO DO THIS BECAUSE

_____

_____

_____

_____

OUR MEMORIES AND THOUGHTS

_____

_____

_____

_____

_____

_____

_____

_____

COMPLETION DATE

_____

WOULD WE DO IT AGAIN?   YES ☐   NO ☐

OUR BUCKET LIST

WE WANT TO DO THIS BECAUSE

OUR MEMORIES AND THOUGHTS

COMPLETION DATE

WOULD WE DO IT AGAIN?   YES ☐   NO ☐

OUR BUCKET LIST

WE WANT TO DO THIS BECAUSE

OUR MEMORIES AND THOUGHTS

COMPLETION DATE

WOULD WE DO IT AGAIN?   YES ☐   NO ☐

OUR BUCKET LIST

WE WANT TO DO THIS BECAUSE

OUR MEMORIES AND THOUGHTS

COMPLETION DATE

WOULD WE DO IT AGAIN?   YES ☐   NO ☐

OUR BUCKET LIST

WE WANT TO DO THIS BECAUSE

OUR MEMORIES AND THOUGHTS

COMPLETION DATE

WOULD WE DO IT AGAIN?   YES ☐   NO ☐

OUR BUCKET LIST

WE WANT TO DO THIS BECAUSE

OUR MEMORIES AND THOUGHTS

COMPLETION DATE

WOULD WE DO IT AGAIN?   YES ☐   NO ☐

OUR BUCKET LIST

WE WANT TO DO THIS BECAUSE

_____

_____

_____

_____

OUR MEMORIES AND THOUGHTS

_____

_____

_____

_____

_____

_____

_____

_____

COMPLETION DATE

_____

WOULD WE DO IT AGAIN?   YES ☐   NO ☐

OUR BUCKET LIST

WE WANT TO DO THIS BECAUSE

_____

_____

_____

_____

OUR MEMORIES AND THOUGHTS

_____

_____

_____

_____

_____

_____

_____

_____

_____

COMPLETION DATE

_____

WOULD WE DO IT AGAIN?   YES ☐   NO ☐

OUR BUCKET LIST

WE WANT TO DO THIS BECAUSE

_____

_____

_____

_____

OUR MEMORIES AND THOUGHTS

_____

_____

_____

_____

_____

_____

_____

_____

COMPLETION DATE

_____

WOULD WE DO IT AGAIN? YES ☐ NO ☐

OUR BUCKET LIST

WE WANT TO DO THIS BECAUSE

OUR MEMORIES AND THOUGHTS

COMPLETION DATE

WOULD WE DO IT AGAIN?   YES ☐   NO ☐

OUR BUCKET LIST

WE WANT TO DO THIS BECAUSE

_____

_____

_____

_____

OUR MEMORIES AND THOUGHTS

_____

_____

_____

_____

_____

_____

_____

_____

_____

COMPLETION DATE

_____

WOULD WE DO IT AGAIN?   YES ☐   NO ☐

OUR BUCKET LIST

WE WANT TO DO THIS BECAUSE

OUR MEMORIES AND THOUGHTS

COMPLETION DATE

WOULD WE DO IT AGAIN?   YES ☐   NO ☐

OUR BUCKET LIST

WE WANT TO DO THIS BECAUSE

_____

_____

_____

_____

OUR MEMORIES AND THOUGHTS

_____

_____

_____

_____

_____

_____

_____

_____

_____

COMPLETION DATE

_____

WOULD WE DO IT AGAIN?   YES ☐   NO ☐

OUR BUCKET LIST

WE WANT TO DO THIS BECAUSE

OUR MEMORIES AND THOUGHTS

COMPLETION DATE

WOULD WE DO IT AGAIN?   YES ☐   NO ☐

OUR BUCKET LIST

WE WANT TO DO THIS BECAUSE

OUR MEMORIES AND THOUGHTS

COMPLETION DATE

WOULD WE DO IT AGAIN?   YES ☐   NO ☐

OUR BUCKET LIST

WE WANT TO DO THIS BECAUSE

OUR MEMORIES AND THOUGHTS

COMPLETION DATE

WOULD WE DO IT AGAIN?   YES ☐   NO ☐

OUR BUCKET LIST

WE WANT TO DO THIS BECAUSE

OUR MEMORIES AND THOUGHTS

COMPLETION DATE

WOULD WE DO IT AGAIN?   YES ☐   NO ☐

OUR BUCKET LIST

WE WANT TO DO THIS BECAUSE

_____

_____

_____

_____

OUR MEMORIES AND THOUGHTS

_____

_____

_____

_____

_____

_____

_____

_____

_____

COMPLETION DATE

_____

WOULD WE DO IT AGAIN?   YES ☐   NO ☐

OUR BUCKET LIST

WE WANT TO DO THIS BECAUSE

_____

_____

_____

_____

OUR MEMORIES AND THOUGHTS

_____

_____

_____

_____

_____

_____

_____

_____

COMPLETION DATE

_____

WOULD WE DO IT AGAIN?   YES ☐   NO ☐

OUR BUCKET LIST

WE WANT TO DO THIS BECAUSE

OUR MEMORIES AND THOUGHTS

COMPLETION DATE

WOULD WE DO IT AGAIN?   YES ☐   NO ☐

OUR BUCKET LIST

WE WANT TO DO THIS BECAUSE

_____

_____

_____

_____

OUR MEMORIES AND THOUGHTS

_____

_____

_____

_____

_____

_____

_____

_____

_____

COMPLETION DATE

_____

WOULD WE DO IT AGAIN?   YES ☐   NO ☐

OUR BUCKET LIST

WE WANT TO DO THIS BECAUSE

_____

_____

_____

_____

OUR MEMORIES AND THOUGHTS

_____

_____

_____

_____

_____

_____

_____

_____

_____

COMPLETION DATE

_____

WOULD WE DO IT AGAIN?   YES ☐   NO ☐

OUR BUCKET LIST

WE WANT TO DO THIS BECAUSE

_____
_____
_____
_____

OUR MEMORIES AND THOUGHTS

_____
_____
_____
_____
_____
_____
_____
_____
_____

COMPLETION DATE

_____

WOULD WE DO IT AGAIN?   YES ☐   NO ☐

OUR BUCKET LIST

WE WANT TO DO THIS BECAUSE

_____
_____
_____
_____

OUR MEMORIES AND THOUGHTS

_____
_____
_____
_____
_____
_____
_____
_____
_____

COMPLETION DATE

_____

WOULD WE DO IT AGAIN? YES ☐ NO ☐

OUR BUCKET LIST

WE WANT TO DO THIS BECAUSE

OUR MEMORIES AND THOUGHTS

COMPLETION DATE

WOULD WE DO IT AGAIN?   YES ☐   NO ☐

OUR BUCKET LIST

WE WANT TO DO THIS BECAUSE

OUR MEMORIES AND THOUGHTS

COMPLETION DATE

WOULD WE DO IT AGAIN?   YES ☐   NO ☐

OUR BUCKET LIST

WE WANT TO DO THIS BECAUSE

_____

_____

_____

_____

OUR MEMORIES AND THOUGHTS

_____

_____

_____

_____

_____

_____

_____

_____

COMPLETION DATE

_____

WOULD WE DO IT AGAIN?   YES ☐   NO ☐

OUR BUCKET LIST

WE WANT TO DO THIS BECAUSE

OUR MEMORIES AND THOUGHTS

COMPLETION DATE

WOULD WE DO IT AGAIN?   YES ☐   NO ☐

OUR BUCKET LIST

WE WANT TO DO THIS BECAUSE

_____

_____

_____

_____

OUR MEMORIES AND THOUGHTS

_____

_____

_____

_____

_____

_____

_____

_____

COMPLETION DATE

_____

WOULD WE DO IT AGAIN?   YES ☐   NO ☐

OUR BUCKET LIST

WE WANT TO DO THIS BECAUSE

_____

_____

_____

_____

OUR MEMORIES AND THOUGHTS

_____

_____

_____

_____

_____

_____

_____

_____

COMPLETION DATE

_____

WOULD WE DO IT AGAIN?   YES ☐   NO ☐

OUR BUCKET LIST

WE WANT TO DO THIS BECAUSE

OUR MEMORIES AND THOUGHTS

COMPLETION DATE

WOULD WE DO IT AGAIN?   YES ☐   NO ☐

OUR BUCKET LIST

WE WANT TO DO THIS BECAUSE

_____
_____
_____
_____

OUR MEMORIES AND THOUGHTS

_____
_____
_____
_____
_____
_____
_____
_____

COMPLETION DATE

_____

WOULD WE DO IT AGAIN?   YES ☐   NO ☐